THE TRUTH IS

1. Leveling up your craft to write a story that lives long after you've left the planet is what some might call a ridiculous goal.

2. You know that you will not tell that story after reading just one how-to-write book.

3. You know that you will not tell that story as the result of taking one seminar.

4. You know that creating a timeless work of art will require the dedication of a world-class athlete. You will be training your mind with as much ferocity and single-minded purpose as an Olympic gold medal hopeful. That kind of cognitive regimen excites you, but you just haven't found a convincing storytelling dojo to do that work.

5. The path to leveling up your creative craft is a dark and treacherous course. You've been at it a long time, and it often feels like you're wearing three-dimensional horse blinders. More times than you'd wish to admit, you're not sure if you are moving north or south or east or west. And the worst part? You can't see anyone else, anywhere going through what you're going through. You're all alone.

WELCOME TO THE STORY GRID UNIVERSE
HERE'S HOW WE CONTEND WITH THOSE TRUTHS

1. We believe we find meaning in the pursuit of creations that last longer than we do. This is *not* ridiculous. Seizing opportunities and overcoming obstacles as we stretch ourselves to reach for seemingly unreachable creations is transformational. We believe this pursuit is the most valuable and honorable way to spend our time here. Even if—especially if—we never reach our lofty creative goals.

2. Writing just one story isn't going to take us to the top. We're moving from point A to Point A^{5000}. We've got lots of mountains to climb, lots of rivers and oceans to cross, and many deep dark forests to traverse along the way. We need topographic guides, and if they're not available, we'll have to figure out how to write them ourselves.

3. We're drawn to seminars to consume the imparted wisdom of an icon in the arena, but we leave with something far more valuable than the curriculum. We get to meet the universe's other pilgrims and compare notes on the terrain.

4. The Story Grid Universe has a virtual dojo, a university in which to work out and get stronger—a place to stumble, correct mistakes, and stumble again, until the moves become automatic and mesmerizing to outside observers.

5. The Story Grid Universe has a performance space, a publishing house dedicated to leveling up the craft with clear boundaries of progress, and the ancillary reference resources to pack for each project mission. There is an infinite number of paths to where you want to be, with a story that works. Seeing how others have made it down their own yellow-brick roads to release their creations into the timeless creative cosmos will help keep you on the straight and narrow path.

All are welcome—the more, the merrier. But please abide by the golden rule:
Put the work above all else, and trust the process.

STORY GRID 101

THE FIVE FIRST PRINCIPLES OF THE STORY
GRID METHODOLOGY

SHAWN COYNE

STORY GRID

Story Grid Publishing LLC
223 Egremont Plain Road
PMB 191
Egremont, MA 01230

Copyright (c) 2020 Story Grid Publishing LLC
Cover Design by Magnus Rex
Edited by Leslie Watts and Shelley Sperry

All Rights Reserved

First Story Grid Publishing Paperback Edition
July 2020

For Information about Special Discounts for Bulk Purchases,
Please visit www.storygridpublishing.com

ISBN: 978-1-64501-023-4
Ebook: 978-1-64501-024-1

For

All Past, Present, and Future Story Nerds

ABOUT THIS BOOK

It's hard to believe it's been five years since I published *The Story Grid: What Good Editors Know*. Since then, I've had the honor of sharing Story Grid tools and methods with thousands of aspiring writers and editors in person and online, and it's turned into a thriving community.

We've spawned three podcasts, in which we discuss and celebrate the craft of writing on a weekly basis. My business partner, client, and friend Tim Grahl and I created a brand-new publishing company as well as online and in-person courses and workshops. We've trained a small army of brilliant writers and editors—all devoted story nerds—who are part of a mutual support society called the Story Grid Guild. It's been a wild and incredibly rewarding ride, with twists that have taken me by surprise, like any great adventure tale.

As our community of storytellers grew larger and more diverse over the past year, we realized the original *Story Grid* book couldn't meet everyone's needs. Thus, we created a book series called Story Grid Beats, in which we present key aspects of the craft in easy-to-digest bites. The topics we cover in the Beats are wide-ranging, and we're adding new volumes on a regular basis.

Recently, we discovered an important piece was missing. With so many books, podcasts, and blog posts on our website now, it can feel overwhelming to writers who are new to our community. We don't want you to feel overwhelmed. We want you to feel welcome. That's why we've written this book as an introduction to Story Grid 101, a sort of gateway into the whole Story Grid way of thinking.

Our goal from the start has been to demystify the art and science of storytelling so anyone who has a story to share—in other words, *everyone*—can learn to write a story that works. Our tools and methods help writers create order out of chaos and build better stories. We try to meet you where you are and show you how to level up your craft.

If you're a beginner looking for exactly where and how to enter the Story Grid world, consider this book your welcome mat and key. Come on in.

WHAT ARE FIRST PRINCIPLES?

If you want to write a great story, you'll encounter challenges along the way. To overcome those, the Story Grid approach relies on a couple of fundamental beliefs.

First, we believe there is a single, overarching story structure that transcends time and cultures and is deeply connected to human cognitive evolution. In fact, the ability to create and share stories is the very stuff that makes us human.

Second, Story Grid is inspired by classical approaches to philosophy, science, and art, including Aristotle's concept of *archai,* or "first principles." First principles are where knowledge starts. Our Story Grid First Principles are the most basic elements of stories—the fundamentals we go back to again and again.

In the following chapters, we'll explore five First Principles and the tools we use to apply those principles. In short, the principles are:

1. Stories are made up of distinct parts, or units.

2. Stories are about change.

3. The change that happens in stories concerns Universal Human Values, the things that most people would say are necessary to survive and thrive in the world—or alternatively, the things that keep us from surviving and thriving.

4. Each unit of story has a Story Event, a one-sentence distillation of what's happening and what value is changing.

5. Within each story unit we find a pattern of change we call the Five Commandments of Storytelling:

- The Inciting Incident, which kicks off the action;
- The Turning Point Complication, which turns the Universal Human Value at stake in the scene;
- The Crisis, which is a big question or dilemma for one of the characters;

- The Climax, which is the decision and action a character takes in response to the Crisis; and
- The Resolution, which is the outcome of the action that happens in the Climax.

The Story Grid tools we'll introduce you to include:

- The Foolscap and Editor's Six Core Questions
- The Spreadsheet
- The Infographic
- The Four Core Framework
- Story's Boundaries

First Principles is for anyone new to Story Grid who needs a primer on how we approach our craft. Writers and editors must understand these principles because they explain the universal structures that support and strengthen every story, no matter the genre or form.

It's not easy to hold all the Story Grid principles, tools, and methods in your head as you work. Even editors who've been immersed in this world for years scramble to look up definitions and examples every day. We hope this book makes all our storytelling a little easier. Leave it on the corner of your desk with Strunk & White and Merriam-Webster, and open it up whenever you need a little help.

1
STORY UNITS

Stories are made up of distinct parts, or units.

Stories are composed of many units, each of which fits into the next like a Russian nesting doll. We need to examine those units to understand how stories work.

The smallest unit of a story, called a *beat* might be only a few words or a few sentences long. The beats combine to create *scenes,* which combine to create *sequences*. Sequences combine to build *acts* and *subplots,* and finally, the *global* story unit, within which all the other units live and interact.

In this book about First Principles, we'll look primarily at the global story unit and one of the smaller units, the scene. Although we'll dig into these two most important units of story here, it's worth knowing a little about each of the other units before we begin.

The smallest unit we study is the beat, a term taken from the performing arts. Actors break down scenes into beats as they explore how their characters change throughout a play or film. A beat is defined by an identifiable change in behavior. Often, it's a brief moment when one character realizes the choice they are making is not working. They're not getting what they want, so they change their tactics. Although it's important for writers to look carefully at each beat in certain critical scenes, most of us shouldn't get distracted by the beats until we've produced a well-crafted manuscript in all other respects.

The next unit of story is the scene. This micro unit is the key to every story that works. Sometimes they're short—a fraction of a chapter—and sometimes long, but in each scene the characters experience movement from Point A to Point B. In a scene that works, a change representing a shift in what we call a *universal human value* takes place. We'll discuss these human values more below.

In both the macro unit of the global story and the micro unit of the scene, we intuitively sense the beginning, middle, and end. And as readers, when we reach the end of a scene, we have the feeling that something has resolved, and it's time to move on to a new bit of action.

The unit of story called a sequence is built with two or more scenes and also has a beginning, middle, and end. Sequences are about critical moments that we sum up in phrases such as "catching the killer," "practicing for the big performance," or "courting the princess." They include a change more significant than what's in a single scene but not the explosive change that happens in an *act*—the next unit in the nesting doll of story.

In the unit of story called the act, the protagonist's life is changed permanently. Not only do the events provide a feeling of resolution for readers, but they also leave us wanting more.

Most novels and films also contain subplots, units of story that amplify or comment on the theme or counterbalance the global story with irony.

The macro, or global, story unit is the whole enchilada. The total experience from start to finish.

We all know what we can expect from a global story when we see a book cover or movie poster because the images are designed to convey that feeling of "horror" or "love" or "war" instantly. The moment we see the iconic movie poster for Jonathan Demme's film, *The*

Silence of the Lambs, based on the novel by Thomas Harris, we know what we're getting. Actress Jodie Foster's face is ghostly, her dark eyes glow, and her mouth is covered by a mysterious insect with a skull across its thorax that foretells death. We sense that a battle between the forces of good and evil will happen in this story—the mark of a classic thriller.

> Why do we bother dividing our stories into all these units?

As writers—and as humans—we can't see both the forest and the trees at the same time. We can't analyze, edit, and polish our macro, or big picture story elements while also analyzing, editing, and polishing our micro, scene-level details. We need to move back and forth so we can see our stories in all their complexity—and tackle the problems one at a time.

The primary tools we use to tackle problems at the global level are the Story Grid Foolscap and Editor's Six Core Questions, the Four Core Framework, and the Story Grid Infographic. You'll find more about each of those in the chapter on Story Grid Tools below. The most valuable tool for analyzing stories at the scene level is the Story Grid Spreadsheet, also explained in the Tools chapter below.

2
CHANGE

Stories are about change.

All stories are about change. The state of the world inside a story and inside each unit of a story is different at the end than it was at the beginning. In fact, the first thing we check when assessing any unit of a story is whether a life-altering change has taken place in the protagonist or another character. The change doesn't always have to be dramatic, but it does have to reflect a real transformation that can be defined in the Story Grid Spreadsheet.

If there is no change in your characters, readers won't care about them. And in the case of the protagonist, the change over the course of the entire story should be irreversible. We expect the characters we care about to take on great challenges and emerge with valuable experiences to share. Stories provide us with knowledge about how to act when we encounter the inevitable conflicts we all face as humans. How we act or don't act when we face such conflicts is the engine of storytelling.

For example, in *The Wonderful Wizard of Oz*, the change at the macro, or global level is about Dorothy gaining maturity and full agency over her life when she confronts frightening challenges far from home. At the micro level, in the first scene, the change is about Dorothy moving from safety to a life in danger as a result of the cyclone.

Examples of Change in Global Stories

In *The Wonderful Wizard of Oz*, Dorothy travels to an extraordinary world and returns a different person, having gained full agency over her life.

In *The Silence of the Lambs*, Clarice Starling is a young FBI trainee who believes the FBI is a meritocracy. By the end of the book, she has become a pro, solved a case that baffled her colleagues, and slain the villain Buffalo Bill. In the process she has changed from a naive trainee to a disillusioned veteran.

In *Pride and Prejudice*, Elizabeth Bennet and Mr. Darcy both lack romantic partners with whom they can form an intimate connection. By the end, they have not only found each other and married but have also made each other better people.

Examples of Change at the Scene Level

In the second scene of *The Wonderful Wizard of Oz*, Dorothy wakes when her little farmhouse lands after the cyclone. She doesn't know where she is or how to get home. The Good Witch of the North suggests she seek help from the Wizard of Oz in the City of Emeralds. In this scene, Dorothy changes from lost and directionless to having a clear direction and goal.

In the second scene of *Pride and Prejudice*, Mrs. Bennet is angry and resentful of Mr. Bennet because he seems to be ignoring their daughters' needs for marriageable young men until she learns he has already visited the new eligible neighbor. In this scene, Mrs. Bennet changes from resentful to delighted.

In the second scene of *The Silence of the Lambs*, Clarice Starling recognizes she's not been chosen to visit Hannibal Lecter because of her merits but is to be used as bait. By the end of the scene, she has forged a relationship with Lecter and he has offered her valuable information. In this scene, Starling changes from thinking she has been chosen for her merits to recognizing she is only bait to feeling chosen once again, this time by Lecter.

3

UNIVERSAL HUMAN VALUES

The change that happens in stories concerns universal human values, the things most people would say are necessary to survive and thrive in the world—or alternatively, the things that keep us from surviving and thriving.

Some positive universal human values include food, shelter, safety, justice, love, respect, knowledge, and self-actualization. The corresponding negative values include hunger, exposure, danger, injustice, hate, disrespect, ignorance, and self-abnegation. If we put these positive human values on one end of a spectrum and their negative opposites on the other end, we can imagine all the variations between as gradations of human experience.

Great stories take into account a broad spectrum of human values, but in all cases, the global story will concern itself and turn on a single human value. Other human values will turn in a global story too, but the core value of the global story will hold sway. We remember *The Silence of the Lambs* as a thriller more than we do as a story about a woman who must change her worldview in order to successfully bring a killer to justice. A worldview value shift has occurred and the justice value has shifted by the end of *The Silence of the Lambs*, but our global feeling, the gestalt of the experience, is that the story was what we have come to know as a thriller.

We evaluate important changes that occur in a scene or global story by focusing on the universal human values at stake. If none of these values changes, it's not a working unit of story.

If we're looking at an Action story, for example, we know change will occur on the Death to Life spectrum. A character could be conscious at the beginning of a scene and unconscious at the end of the scene. That's a change in a universal human value and helps us define the scene as a working unit of story.

You'll find an introduction to value changes in Story Grid editor Valerie Francis's article,

"Value Shift 101," here: https://storygrid.com/value-shift-101/.

Universal Human Values: Global and Scene-Level Examples

The Wonderful Wizard of Oz

Because it's an Action story, the global spectrum of human values is Death to Life.

- In the first scene, the universal human value shifts from Life to Possible Death, or positive to negative, when Toto leaps out of Dorothy's arms to hide under the bed as the cyclone approaches.
- In the second scene, the universal human value shifts from Safe to Lost to Directed when the Good Witch seeks advice on Dorothy's behalf and learns that she should go to the City of Emeralds.

Pride and Prejudice

Because it's a Love story (in the Courtship subgenre), the global spectrum of human values is from Hate to Love, or more specifically, from Hate to Commitment.

- In the first scene, the universal human value shifts from Hope to Despair, a shift from positive to negative, when Mr. Bennet refuses to visit Mr. Bingley, a potential mate for one of his daughters.
- In the second scene, the universal human value shifts from Resentful to Delighted, a shift from negative to positive, when Mr. Bennet reports he has met Mr. Bingley and his daughters will soon meet the young man.

The Silence of the Lambs

Because it's a Thriller, the global spectrum of human values is Damnation to Life.

- In the first scene, the value changes from Ignored to Chosen when Crawford offers Starling an important assignment. This moves the value from negative to positive.
- In the second scene, the value changes from Chosen for Merit to Used as Bait to Chosen again when

a naive Clarice Starling realizes how the reality of FBI life differs from her fantasy. Then she encounters Lecter and he offers her some valuable information. Notice that the value starts as positive, moves to the negative, and then ends positive, though less so than when the scene began.

4

STORY EVENT

Each unit of Story has a Story Event, a one-sentence distillation of what's happening and what value is changing.

If *the Story Grid* method is like an MRI scan, it should give us the ability to find our story problems quickly. We should be able to use it to immediately find broken story bones or damaged story tissue. We create this scan by summing up thousands of words of a story unit into a single phrase or sentence. We call this phrase or sentence the Story Event. Below, we'll look at Story Events at the scene level, first looking at *The Wonderful Wizard of Oz,* and then at *Pride and Prejudice* and *The Silence of the Lambs*.

We use four questions to help us generate our Story Event:

1. What are the characters literally doing? That is, what are their micro on-the-ground actions?

Are they going on a walk? Are they blasting off for Mars? Are they running from a monster? You don't have to overthink this one. Simply write down what is literally happening. In the first scene of *The Wonderful Wizard of Oz*:

> *Uncle Henry, Dorothy, and Auntie Em see an impending cyclone and prepare for its arrival.*

2. What is the essential tactic of the characters? That is, what macro behaviors are they employing that are linked to a universal human value?

Figuring out the essential tactic is a bit trickier. We do a lot of things automatically, without thinking about why. Digging into the essential tactic of a character will require you to think about the things we do and the way we do them to get what we want and need in the world. Here are just a few common essential tactics:

- To convince a friend to take a big step

- To assure a loved one of our devotion
- To get a liar to admit the truth
- To sell someone on a great idea
- To seduce someone
- To humiliate someone

In the first scene of *The Wonderful Wizard of Oz*:

Uncle Henry safeguards the livestock, Dorothy safeguards Toto, and Auntie Em safeguards herself.

3. What universal human values have changed for one or more characters in the scene? Which one of those value changes is most important and should be included in the Story Grid Spreadsheet?

After we have a sense of what happens (what the characters are literally doing) and the essential tactics of the characters inside that Story Event (what they are really trying to get from another character), we'll be able to figure out what universal human value changed from the beginning of the scene to the end. In the first scene of *The Wonderful Wizard of Oz*:

All the characters' lives are threatened. The

value changes from life to possible death for all of them.

Identifying the most important value change in a scene is sometimes difficult. This scene begins "on the ground" and ends, quite literally, in the air, which threatens the life of the protagonist. The choice is clear. We'll track Life to Death in the value shift column of the spreadsheet.

When in doubt, the Story Grid rule of thumb is to highlight the value that best aligns with the progress of the human value at stake in the global story. *The Wonderful Wizard of Oz* is an Action story, which has a global value at stake on the Death to Life spectrum. Throughout the Story Grid Spreadsheet, we'll track the ways life is threatened or supported scene by scene.

4. What Story Event sums up the scene's on-the-ground actions, essential tactics, and value change? We will enter that event in the Story Grid Spreadsheet.

After we've completed the analysis of the scene, we can use our answers to construct a one-sentence Story Event description. In the first scene of *The Wonderful Wizard of Oz*, the Story Event we can put on our spreadsheet is:

A cyclone lifts a one-room Kansas farmhouse off of the ground with a little orphan girl and her dog still inside.

Finding the Story Event in Scene 1 of *Pride and Prejudice*

1. What are the characters literally doing? That is, what are their micro on-the-ground actions?

   Mrs. Bennet shares the latest news from the neighborhood with her husband.

2. What is the essential tactic of the characters? That is, what macro behaviors are they employing that are linked to a universal human value?

   Mrs. Bennet is trying to get Mr. Bennet to seize a great opportunity for their daughters. But Mr. Bennet is trying to have a bit of fun at his wife's expense.

3. What universal human values have changed for one or more characters in the scene? Which one of those value changes is most important and should be included in the Story Grid Spreadsheet?

> *Mr. Bennet's enjoyment turns to annoyance when his wife reminds him of his duty to his daughters. Mrs. Bennet's hope that she can get one of her five daughters married turns to despair when her husband refuses to visit an attractive prospective son-in-law. Because the global genre is Love story, and Mrs. Bennet is trying to bring lovers together, Hope to Despair is the best choice for the value change.*

4. What Story Event sums up the scene's on-the-ground actions, essential tactics, and value change? We will enter that event in the Story Grid Spreadsheet.

> *Mr. Bennet refuses his wife's request that he visit a rich eligible bachelor.*

Finding the Story Event in Scene 1 of *The Silence of the Lambs*

1. What are the characters literally doing? That is, what are their micro on-the-ground actions?

> *FBI Section Chief Jack Crawford and Clarice Starling are having a conversation in his office.*

2. What is the essential tactic of the characters? That is, what macro behaviors are they employing that are linked to a universal human value?

> *Starling wants to make a good impression. Crawford wants to manipulate Starling into doing a dangerous task.*

3. What universal human values have changed for one or more characters in the scene? Which one of those value changes is most important and should be included in the Story Grid Spreadsheet?

> *Crawford shifts from having no options to having a good option, but also from a mentor to an exploiter. Starling's universal human value shifts from ignored to chosen when Crawford offers the assignment. Ignored to Chosen is the value change we add to the spreadsheet.*

4. What Story Event sums up the scene's on-the-ground actions, essential tactics, and value change? We will enter that event in the Story Grid Spreadsheet.

> *FBI trainee Clarice Starling is summoned*

by FBI Section Chief Jack Crawford and assigned an "interesting errand."

For more help in crafting scenes that really work, take a look at "Essential Action: The Key to Compelling Characterization," by Anne Hawley and Leslie Watts, which is available here: https://storygrid.com/essential-action-key-compelling-characterization/. You'll also find some great tips in "Building Better Scenes," a *Story Grid Podcast* episode here: https://storygrid.com/one-scene-at-a-time/.

5

FIVE COMMANDMENTS

Within each story unit we find a pattern of change we call the Five Commandments of Storytelling.

Now that we know about Universal Human Values, Story Events, and how to identify the value shift so you can boil down thousands of words of narrative into a single sentence or phrase, we can take a look at the final First Principle, which is one you'll apply every time you sit down to sketch out a beat or scene or a Foolscap for an entire novel. In this principle, we incorporate patterns of change in our stories by identifying the Five Commandments of Storytelling:

- The Inciting Incident, which kicks off the action;
- The Turning Point Progressive Complication (also called the Phere), an unexpected event that turns the human value at stake in the scene and gives rise to ...
- The Crisis, which is a dilemma about how to confront the unexpected event;
- The Climax, which is the decision and action a character takes in response to the Crisis; and
- The Resolution, which is the outcome of the action of the Climax.

Commandment 1: Inciting Incident

You must have an inciting incident. It should be based on a change in a universal human value. Something happens that leads to an imbalance in the life of your protagonist or group of protagonists, and that leads the character(s) to adopt the goal they'll pursue throughout the story or unit of story. The incident could be as simple as waking up in the morning or as complex as being served legal papers for an upcoming divorce at breakfast.

In the first scene of *The Wonderful Wizard of Oz*, the inciting incident is: A cyclone approaches a one-room farmhouse on the wide-open Kansas plains.

Commandment 2: Turning Point Progressive Complication (Phere)

Progressive complications happen when something in the environment responds to the protagonist or point of view character's pursuit of a goal. The complications could be obstacles that stand in the way of achieving the goal or tools that help achieve the goal. One particular complication, an unexpected event, allows the character to make sense of the inciting incident in a new way. It might be an action or a revelation in the mind of the character. This is the turning point progressive complication. We now often refer to this as the "phere" because it's like an unexpected "ball of chaos," much like the golden snitch in J.K. Rowling's Harry Potter novels. The phere creates a situation that keeps the protagonist from reaching their goal in the way they'd planned, sparking the crisis.

In the first scene of *The Wonderful Wizard of Oz,* the turning point progressive complication, or phere, happens when Toto the dog leaps from Dorothy's arms as she moves toward the cellar door and safety. Toto's unexpected disobedience is the active turn in the story that changes the life value from safe and alive to in danger and close to death.

Commandment 3: Crisis

You must have a crisis. To put it simply, a crisis boils down to an either/or question—a dilemma—that might be large or small depending on the story unit but forces a choice. The character will have to choose between two negative options (a best bad choice) or between options that may be good for one party and bad for another (irreconcilable goods choice).

In the first scene of *The Wonderful Wizard of Oz,* the crisis is a best bad choice. If Dorothy turns back to fetch Toto, it's likely that she will endanger herself. If she doesn't, Toto is certain to die.

Commandment 4: Climax

You must have a climax. The climax of a story is the decision and action the character takes when faced with their best bad choice or irreconcilable goods choice.

In the first scene of *The Wonderful Wizard of Oz,* the climax is: Dorothy rescues Toto.

Commandment 5: Resolution

You must have a resolution. A resolution happens in the environment as a result of the climactic action. We always need to know the result of the choice.

In the first scene of *The Wonderful Wizard of Oz,* the resolution is that the farmhouse is lifted off the ground by the cyclone with Dorothy and Toto still inside.

The Five Commandments in Scene 1 of *The Silence of the Lambs*

- Inciting Incident: Section Chief Jack Crawford summons Starling, an FBI trainee, to his office.
- Turning Point Progressive Complication (Phere): Crawford offers Starling the assignment to interview Dr. Hannibal Lecter.
- Crisis: Best Bad Choice. Does she agree to the assignment or decline? If she declines, she probably won't get another assignment, but if she accepts, she will be vulnerable to a dangerous serial killer.
- Climax: Starling accepts the assignment.
- Resolution: Crawford explains

details of Lecter's cases, warns Starling not to deviate from procedure, and tells her she wasn't chosen at random.

The Five Commandments in Scene 1 of *Pride and Prejudice*

- Inciting Incident: A bachelor has rented a nearby manor.
- The Turning Point Progressive Complication (Phere): Social convention requires the family to be formally introduced; the Bennet girls cannot meet Mr. Bingley until their father does and Mr. Bennet is showing no interest in making the man's acquaintance, which is entirely unexpected given the prospects for his unmarried daughters.
- Crisis: Irreconcilable Goods Choice. Mr. Bennet can continue to enjoy his private time or agree to go meet Mr. Bingley.
- Climax: Mr. Bennet refuses to visit Mr. Bingley.
- Resolution: The Bennet daughters will have no opportunity to meet Mr. Bingley.

You'll find many more resources that explore the Five Commandments on the Story Grid website. A few that will get you started are "The Five Commandments of Storytelling," here: https://storygrid.com/5-commandments/, "The Five Commandments of storytelling (Revisited)," on the podcast here: https://storygrid.com/5-commandments-storytelling-revisited/, and "A Deeper Dive into the Five Commandments of storytelling," here: https://storygrid.com/a-deeper-dive-into-the-five-commandments-of-storytelling/.

And for an introduction to the concept of the "phere," check out: "5 Commandments and Pheres," here: https://storygrid.com/5-commandments-and-pheres/.

STORY GRID TOOLS

As story nerds through and through, we have our own version of tech nerds' cool gadgets and gizmos. Our Story Grid tools help us analyze and improve our writing. There is an array to choose from, and some you'll find more useful for early drafts while others help most in the editing process. Here is a quick inventory of the toolbox:

The Foolscap and Editor's Six Core Questions

The Foolscap and the Editor's Six Core Questions are among the first Story Grid tools any writer or editor makes use of. A "Foolscap" is an old-fashioned term for a yellow legal pad of paper. According to author Steven Pressfield, a single Foolscap page is the perfect amount of space for sketching out the essential outline of any story. This is how we suggest writers begin, even if you prefer to write "by the seat of your pants" with no strict outline.

To make building that essential outline easier, you can ask yourself six questions and record the answers on the page. These happen to be the first questions a Story Grid editor will consider when evaluating your story, so the writer's Foolscap and the Editor's Six Core Questions are identical. The questions, with brief explanations, are:

1. What's the global genre?

Story Grid puts all stories into content genres, similar to but not precisely the same as the sales categories we see on Amazon or in brick-and-mortar stores. We separate stories into nine *external* genres and three *internal* genres, which we discuss a bit more in the next section. You'll find links to detailed discussions of the genres, with "cheat sheets" for each, in the article, "Genres of Writing: What Are They? Why Do They Matter?" here: https://storygrid.com/genres-of-writing/.

2. What are the conventions and obligatory events for your genre?

Conventions are the elements of a particular

genre that must appear in a story to set up reader expectations. A mystery must have an investigator—whether professional or amateur—to solve a crime, for example.

Obligatory events are required to pay off reader expectations in a particular genre. A murder mystery must include a scene in which someone discovers the dead body.

Although at first glance, the conventions and obligatory events appear to be a simple list of items to include in stories of a particular genre, it's not really a list, but a *tool* that enhances your ability to show readers the global pattern of change. You'll learn much of what you need to know about conventions and obligatory events in the article, "Genres Have Conventions and Obligatory Scenes" at https://storygrid.com/genres-have-conventions-and-obligatory-scenes/ and in Story Grid editor Kim Kessler's presentation, "Conventions and Obligatory Scenes," which you can listen to or read here: https://storygrid.com/editor-roundtable-conventions-obligatory-scenes/.

3. What are the point of view (POV) and narrative device?

The POV and narrative device combine to establish the vantage point you use to tell the reader your story and dictate the tenor of each scene. We're all familiar with first person, second person, and third person POVs. In *Pride and Prejudice*, like many nineteenth-century authors, Jane Austen uses primarily the third-person omniscient point of view. Thomas Harris employs the powerful combination of first and third person in *The Silence of the Lambs*. This allows Harris into the thoughts of the protagonist and several other characters, a valuable tool in a thriller.

We also need to consider the narrative device that is the bridge between the minds of the author and the reader. For example, does that connection take the form of a diary, a fictional autobiography, or stream-of-consciousness? The POV and narrative device must work together because they determine *how* you present that story to your readers. If they are not in sync, you'll undermine your story.

You'll find helpful articles about POV on the Story Grid website, including "Consider the Source: Elements of Point of View and Narrative Device," here: https://storygrid.com/consider-the-source-pov/ and "Choosing Your Point of View," here: https://storygrid.com/choosing-your-pov/.

4. What are the objects of desire?

If you know your genre, you've probably already figured out your protagonist's objects of desire, whether those are external wants or internal needs. Objects of desire drive the actions of other characters in your story too, especially the external antagonist. Identifying what characters want helps you understand what actions they will take to achieve their desires.

Wants are your character's conscious desires and goals, the things they believe they're on a journey to get. These wants are typically connected directly to the external content genre of your story. For example, in *Pride and Prejudice,* a Courtship Love story, Elizabeth Bennet wants to marry a true gentleman and rejects those who fall short.

Needs are your character's subconscious desires, what they truly require in order to complete their journey. Needs are typically dictated by the internal content genre of your story. Elizabeth Bennet's journey toward marriage (the classic resolution of a Courtship Love story) is really about her need for a mature, sophisticated understanding of love. The internal content genre of *Pride and Prejudice* is Worldview-Maturation.

A helpful place to find further information about objects of desire is the article, "Story Fuel," here: https://storygrid.com/story-fuel/.

Also take a look at Story Grid editor Anne Hawley's talk and article on the topic here: https://storygrid.com/editor-roundtable-objects-of-desire/ and the article by former Story Grid editor Larry Pass, "Objects of Desire, Objects of Conflict," here: https://storygrid.com/objects-of-desire/.

5. What's the controlling idea/theme?

The takeaway message that you want your reader to discover is your story's controlling idea or theme. Let's be clear, few writers really know what this is at the start, so be patient. When you finally understand the theme that animates the characters and their choices, the story often comes to life in new ways.

Ideally, the controlling idea will be boiled down to very few words, and no more than a sentence. It should describe the global value change and should be as specific as possible about what causes that change. It often seems a bit too simple, but that's the point.

The controlling idea of *The Wonderful Wizard of Oz* is: "Life's meaning reveals itself as we seize our individual agency and ceaselessly pursue a return to our vision of 'home.'"

The controlling idea of *Pride and Prejudice* is: "Love triumphs when we dispel base attitudes and embrace the vibrant mix of humanity among all social classes."

And for *The Silence of the Lambs,* it's: "Life prevails when the hero identifies with the vulnerability of the victims as deeply as she understands the core pathology of the villain."

You'll find discussions of the controlling idea in "The Big Takeaway," here: https://storygrid.com/the-big-takeaway/ and in Story Grid editor Savannah Gilbo's article, "Theme of a Story: 3 Ways to Uncover Yours," here: https://storygrid.com/theme/.

6. What is the Beginning Hook, Middle Build, and Ending Payoff?

The last item you need on your handy Foolscap page is a concise explanation of the three acts of your story—the beginning hook, middle build (which can be broken into two parts), and ending payoff. For the beginning hook, you'll sum up the challenge or problem the protagonist faces. For the middle build, you'll sum up how the stakes are raised and how the tension builds for your protagonist on their journey. For the ending payoff, you'll sum up the climax of the global story, or how the protagonist ultimately faces the challenge or solves the problem.

In the Editor's Six Core Questions, we tend

to sum things up in just a sentence. But when we create a Foolscap, we like to include the Five Commandments in each section.

As an example, let's look at the simplest, one-sentence summaries of hook, build, and payoff for *The Silence of the Lambs:*

- Beginning Hook: Clarice Starling gets a job to interview Hannibal Lecter.
- Middle Build: Hannibal Lecter escapes.
- Ending Payoff: Clarice Starling catches and kills Buffalo Bill.

Finally, for a hefty dose of inspiration, you'll find the Foolscaps for *The Wonderful Wizard of Oz* here: https://storygrid.com/masterwork/wizardofoz, for *Pride and Prejudice* here: https://storygrid.com/resources/Foolscap-global-story-grid-pride-and-prejudice/, and for *The Silence of the Lambs* here: https://storygrid.com/wp-content/uploads/2015/03/FINAL-PAGE-289.jpg

The Twelve Content Genres

As you're working on your Foolscap, before you do anything else, you'll need to consider what kind of story you want to tell. The type, or *genre,* will depend on your protagonist's wants and needs. Story Grid divides stories into twelve distinct content genres. Nine are *external* and based on your protagonist's wants. Those external genres are Action, War, Horror, Crime, Thriller, Western, Love, Performance, and Society. The three *internal* content genres—Status, Morality, and Worldview—are defined by your protagonist's deeper, internal needs.

The Wonderful Wizard of Oz belongs in the Action story genre, with an internal Worldview-Maturation genre. *The Silence of the Lambs* is a Thriller with an internal genre of Worldview-Disillusionment. And of course, *Pride and Prejudice* is a Love story, with an internal genre of Worldview-Maturation.

We have plenty of articles on the Story Grid website that can help you identify your genres (both internal and external) if you're having trouble. A good place to start is "Genres of Writing: What are They? Why Do They Matter?" at https://storygrid.com/genres-of-writing/. A helpful tool that we use to translate your protagonist's needs into the proper genre is the Story Grid Gas Gauge of Need, downloadable here: https://storygrid.com/resources/story-grid-gas-gauge-of-need/

The Spreadsheet

One of the defining tools of the Story Grid approach to editing is our Story Grid Spreadsheet. We put details of our scenes into a spreadsheet to keep track of all the information when we analyze books, screenplays, and even longform articles. For story nerds, there's nothing more exciting than compiling the data and discovering how a story is constructed from the inside out, top to bottom. It's like an MRI scan for your book. We won't go over each column and data point here, but some of the vital information for each and every scene includes word count, Story Event, value shift, turning point progressive complication (phere), point of view, period of time, duration, location, onstage and offstage characters mentioned.

To understand the value of the spreadsheet, it helps to review one for a masterwork. You'll find a full Story Grid Spreadsheet for *The Wonderful Wizard of Oz* here: https://storygrid.com/masterwork/wizardofoz, for *Pride and Prejudice* here: https://storygrid.com/resources/story-grid-spreadsheet-pride-and-prejudice/, and for *The Silence of the Lambs* here: https://storygrid.com/resources/story-grid-spreadsheet-silence-of-the-lambs/.

If we look at the spreadsheet of *The Silence*

of the Lambs, we discover a wealth of information we wouldn't notice with any other tool. We see the variation in the length and duration of scenes that keeps the pace exciting and unpredictable. We see which characters appear most often, with whom, and where. We also see the turning point (phere) and value shift for each scene.

By looking at details of the first four scenes of *The Silence of the Lambs,* we see how rapidly protagonist Clarice Starling's fortunes rise and fall, which helps to draw readers in and elicits their sympathy for her immediately. The value shifts in these scenes move her 1) from ignored as a novice agent in training to chosen for a special assignment; 2) from chosen for her merits to being used as bait by her bosses; 3) from an unwanted to a welcome guest of Hannibal Lecter; and 4) from encouraged by the opportunity she's had to discouraged when rebuffed by her boss.

Looking at other aspects of the spreadsheet we see that Thomas Harris has squeezed a lot of action into just two days' time, and we note that he's also introduced seven onstage characters and an army of offstage characters. It's easy to see how powerful this tool can be and why we call it an MRI for your story, isn't it? The spreadsheet will reveal the skeleton and muscles holding your scenes together as well as any broken bones or wounds that need fixing.

Scene Analysis and Story Events

After counting the number of words in a scene, the first item we usually need to put into the Story Grid Spreadsheet is a summary of the scene, called a Story Event. As we mentioned in Principle 4 above, a Story Event is simply a short description of the active change in a scene. We use our Scene Analysis Tools, in the form of our four questions (also discussed above), to find that key Story Event. Here's a quick example of how we discover the Story Event in another scene from *Pride and Prejudice,* in which Elizabeth Bennet and Mr. Darcy decide to marry.

1. What are the characters literally doing? That is, what are their micro on-the-ground actions?

Darcy and Elizabeth go for a walk.

2. What is the essential tactic of the characters? That is, what macro behaviors are they employing that are linked to a universal human value?

> *The two lovers confess their love and true feelings for one another.*

3. What universal human values have changed for one or more characters in the scene? Which one of those value changes is most important and should be included in the Story Grid Spreadsheet?

> *Elizabeth has gone from Depressed because she believes her love is unrequited and can never be fulfilled to Overjoyed because Darcy returns her affection.*

4. What Story Event sums up the scene's on-the-ground actions, essential tactics, and value change? We will enter that event in the Story Grid Spreadsheet.

> *When Darcy and Bingley come to Longbourn, Elizabeth declares her feelings for Darcy and he returns those feelings, leading to a joyful reunion.*

The Infographic

There's another Story Grid tool to mention—one that allows us to link insights on the macro and micro levels, bringing together all the information we have in one visual snapshot. It's the Story Grid Infographic. The infographic charts the progression of time and each scene along the X-axis, and the global values at stake in both the internal and external genres on the Y-axis.

You'll find the infographic for *The Wonderful Wizard of Oz* here: https://storygrid.com/masterwork/wizardofoz, for *Pride and Prejudice* here: https://storygrid.com/resources/story-grid-graph-pride-and-prejudice/, and for *The Silence of the Lambs* here: https://storygrid.com/resources/silence-of-the-lambs-story-grid/.

The Four Core Framework

One of the most helpful additions to our story toolbox recently is the Four Core Framework, laid out in detail in a book by the same name. The framework is based on the expectations readers have for each content genre. If a writer can satisfy those expectations, readers will be delighted and want more (and tell their friends about it). Story Grid can help you answer questions about reader expectations by bringing the *core* of your story into focus. The core makes a story irresistible, memorable, and worth sharing by providing readers with a cathartic emotional moment. Each of the elements that make up the Four Core

Framework supports the others, and they all work together to determine whether readers walk away satisfied. Those elements, with examples from *Pride and Prejudice,* are:

- **The Core Need** (survival or esteem, for example). Elizabeth Bennet and Mr. Darcy share the core need for *connection*. That need awakens when they meet and requires that both become vulnerable and better versions of themselves before they can attain that need.
- **The Core Life Values** (a range from life to death or impotence to power, for example). The life values at stake in *Pride and Prejudice* range from hate to love, with many gradations on that spectrum.
- **The Core Emotion** (excitement or admiration, for example) that we as readers want when we choose a Love story is *romance.* If Elizabeth and Darcy can find authentic connection, perhaps we can too. And their story shows us that love matters because it makes us better people.
- **The Core Event** (a battle scene or a showdown between the protagonist

and antagonist, for example). The core event is the "proof of love" scene in which Darcy sacrifices to help Elizabeth and her family. Through this event the connection between the two lovers becomes exponentially stronger.

Story's Boundaries

We've examined stories from many angles using lots of tools and examples so far, but there's one final Story Grid tool we are continually developing. It brings us full circle back to looking at the global unit of story.

We believe that no matter the setting, theme, or characters, every story happens within boundaries that correspond to two kinds of change. We say these limits exist "on the ground" and "in the clouds," and they are represented by two of our global content genres—the primal Action story and the transcendent Worldview story. In other words, Action and Worldview represent the external and internal boundaries of story respectively. And all of the other genres live in a space between them.

Externally, every protagonist must *act* to create change in their environment, or *on the ground*. This is the *Action* component of every story. Dorothy Gale acts to defeat the witch and get home. Elizabeth Bennet acts to find a proper husband. Clarice Starling acts to catch a killer. Characters enact internally formed tactics to further their global strategies to achieve long term goals. That's how they pursue what they want. They actualize motor movements to move from point A (an unfulfilled goal) to Point Z (a fulfilled goal) and either succeed or fail in those pursuits.

Internally, when the protagonist tries to solve the problem presented by the inciting incident of their story, they rely on their existing knowledge base. But when unexpected events arise, their bedrock of knowledge breaks down and is found wanting. The protagonist must accept failure or transform the way they *see* the problem—transcending their current understanding by rising to a vantage point *in the clouds* where they can *break their own cognitive frame.* This is the transcendent *Worldview* component of every story. The character must transcend their state of being and level up to a higher state to solve the dilemma. Alternatively, they fail to do so and cling to their state as is or cognitively spiral downward.

Breaking the cognitive frame isn't as simple as "thinking outside the box" or seeing a problem from a new angle. Instead, the protagonist recognizes their current frame, or way of understanding the world, isn't up to the task of solving their problem. Something entirely new is called for. So Dorothy changes how she sees her own agency. Elizabeth redefines a good marriage. And Clarice loses faith in the institutions of justice so she can embody justice.

CONCLUSION

We hope we've provided a portal into the world of Story Grid that helps you understand our First Principles and how they can—along with our toolbox of Foolscap, Spreadsheet, Infographic, and more—help you write the stories you've always wanted to write.

If one sentence sums up why we care so much about stories and why we built the Story Grid community, it's this:

Stories create meaning in our lives and change in the world.

We're all on our own version of a heroic journey, trying to figure out what our gifts are so we can survive, thrive, find meaning, and leave something of value behind. As writers and editors, we want to leave behind our stories.

If you'd like to know more, we invite you to join our community through our books, courses, and the Story Grid Guild. You'll find all the information you need at https://storygrid.com.

ABOUT THE AUTHOR

SHAWN COYNE created, developed, and expanded the story analysis and problem-solving methodology the Story Grid during his quarter-century-plus career in book publishing. A seasoned story editor, book publisher, and ghostwriter, Coyne has also co-authored *The Ones Who Hit the Hardest: The Steelers, the Cowboys, the '70s, and the Fight For America's Soul* with Chad Millman and *Cognitive Dominance: A Brain Surgeon's Quest to Out-Think Fear* with Mark McLaughlin, M.D. With his friend and editorial client Steven Pressfield, Coyne runs Black Irish Entertainment, publisher of the cult classic book *The War of Art*. Coyne oversees the Story Grid Universe, which includes Story Grid University and Story Grid Publishing, with his friend and editorial client Tim Grahl.

www.ingramcontent.com/pod-product-compliance
Lightning Source LLC
Chambersburg PA
CBHW051039030426
42336CB00015B/2950